ROOTED
in Faith

ROOTED
in Faith

A Teen's Guide to Getting to Know
God and Growing Real Faith

ELLEN ANNE KLEIN

Dedication

To the next generation searching for something real.
I pray you find that faith isn't about religion; it's about a
relationship.

To the friends and family who have stood with me through
every season of life . . .
I wish I'd had a guide like this to ground me sooner.
You definitely would have enjoyed a better version of me.

And most of all, to the God who never stopped pursuing me,
thank You for turning every question, mistake, and heartache
into grace.

Contents

Introduction

Hey there; I'm so glad you're here.

If you're reading this, something inside you wants
to understand faith in a real way, not the surface
kind that fades when life gets messy, but the kind
that holds steady when everything else shakes.

I get it. I've been there.
For a long time, I believed in God, but I didn't *know*
Him. I thought being a Christian was mostly about
rules, prayers, and doing the right thing. But what
I didn't realize was that faith isn't a checklist; it's a
relationship.

That's why I wrote *Rooted in Faith.*

It's not a lecture.
It's not a list of dos and don'ts.
It's a conversation, the kind we'd have if we were
sitting together over coffee, talking about the
questions you've been carrying for a while but
maybe never said out loud.

Because here's the truth:
Faith grows best when it's real.

When it's personal.
When you're honest about your doubts and still
show up anyway.

This book isn't about being "perfect."
It's about learning to walk with God
in the middle of *real life.*
School, friends, family, decisions, heartbreaks,
pressure . . . all of it.

So wherever you are in your faith right now,
curious, confused, brand new, or
rebuilding, this is a safe place to start.
You don't need to have it all figured out.
You just need to take one small step closer.

That's how roots grow, little by little, deeper and
stronger over time.

You can read this book straight through or
jump around to what speaks to you most.
There's no wrong way to start.

Just start.

A Note Before You Begin

Faith isn't about pretending to have all the answers.
It's about knowing where to take your questions.
So if you ever feel lost, uncertain,
or unqualified, remember:

God isn't asking for perfection.
He's inviting you into a relationship that changes everything.

Ready?

Let's dig in and start growing, one chapter, one truth, one step at a time.

I Believed in God . . . But I Didn't Know Him

If I could go back and talk to the younger me,
I wouldn't start with rules or a list of expectations.
I'd start with a story . . .
the one where I thought I understood faith,
but really, I didn't.

I believed in God.
I knew about church,
prayer before dinner,
and trying to be a "good person."

But I didn't understand
that faith isn't something you attend.
It's something you live.

No one failed to teach me.
I just couldn't hear it yet.
I thought religion was about showing up,
not growing close.
It never crossed my mind

that what God wanted
wasn't my surface faith;
it was my relationship.

I thought I knew what was important:
be kind,
work hard,
try your best,
hope it all works out.
But without realizing it,
I was coasting,
trying to do life in my own strength,
filling my days with effort and good intentions,
but wondering why peace never stayed very long.

When faith is absent,
you work hard to hold everything together.
You manage stress,
hide worry,
fight off jealousy,
wrestle with comparison and conflict,
and think that's just life.

But the truth is,
you're running on empty.

I didn't know I was missing anything
because I didn't know there was something
more to have.

I believed in God . . . yes . . .
but I didn't know how to build my life on Him.
I didn't have a belief problem.
I had a relationship problem.

The first time I truly turned to God
wasn't planned.

It happened on one of those days
that leaves you feeling like
you've reached the edge of yourself,
the place where strength runs out
and desperation settles in.

So, I did something instinctively . . .
something without realizing why.
I reached for the Bible.
(Actually, I had to find it first.)

There it sat,
on a shelf,
our old family Bible.

It wasn't the kind you read from.
It was the kind that held stories of its own.

Oversized.
Heavy.
Its pages soft and fragile
from years of being opened
for reasons other than Scripture.

Inside were pressed flowers,
bits of life preserved between verses,
and my mother's beautiful handwriting,
carefully recording births, marriages, and deaths.

Up until that moment,
I had never opened it to read the words inside.
To me, it had always been a record of our family,
not a conversation with God.

I reached for it. . . .
Not because I knew what I was doing.
Not because I had a verse in mind.
Not because I understood Scripture.

I just knew I needed His Word
more than I needed anything else.

I opened the Bible without a plan.
I didn't know where to turn.
I didn't even understand what I was reading.
But I started reading it out loud.

Not to be religious.
Not to impress God.
Not because I "felt spiritual."

But because in that moment . . .
I knew the answer wasn't in me.
The answer was in Him.
His Word was my only weapon.

And even if I didn't fully "get it,"
as tears streamed down my face,
I could feel that something was happening
as I spoke it.

Even though I didn't fully understand,
I sensed I was where I needed to be.

The words didn't just fill the space;
they filled *me*.

I didn't realize it at the time . . .
but I was in the midst of spiritual warfare.

The battle between good and evil.
I was fighting back.

Every word I read out loud
felt like I was pushing back the darkness.
I wasn't just trying to "feel better."
I was standing my ground.

And the crazy part?
I still didn't understand what I was reading.
But I didn't need to.

Because the power wasn't in my understanding.
The power was in His Word.

For the first time . . .
I wasn't just believing in God from a distance.
I was depending on Him.

Faith stopped being an idea
and started becoming a lifeline.

And slowly, I began to understand what Jesus
was teaching in Scripture.

That when you hear His words
and begin to live them,
you're building your life on something solid
(see **Matthew 7:24**).

Faith isn't about knowing every answer.
It's about knowing the One you can trust
when nothing makes sense.

It's the steady ground beneath your feet
when everything else shifts.

Can I Really Trust the Bible?

I didn't realize it at the time,
but what I was holding wasn't just a book of
stories; it was the living Word of God.
Every page was written with purpose,
breathed out by the One who spoke the
universe into existence.

> *"All Scripture is God-breathed and is*
> *useful for teaching, rebuking, correcting*
> *and training in righteousness."*
> *— 2 Timothy 3:16*

That verse reminds me the Bible isn't outdated
or irrelevant;
it's alive.
It still speaks because truth doesn't expire.
Even when I didn't understand what I was reading,
I was taking in God's truth.
Every word was planting something inside me.
The power wasn't in my understanding;
it was in His Word.

Once you start reading the Bible not as a rule book
but as a conversation,
you begin to hear God speaking personally,
guiding, comforting, convicting, and
reminding you that He is near.

Taking a Step of Faith

Faith doesn't begin with having all the answers.
It begins with a single step,
a choice to trust God
in the middle of what you don't understand.

Sometimes that step looks small:
opening your Bible,
whispering a prayer,
choosing to listen instead of rush.

But small steps lead to solid ground.
And each time you turn toward God,
your roots grow deeper.
Your trust grows stronger.
Your peace becomes real.

You don't have to wait
for life to make sense
to start walking with Him.
He meets you right where you are,
and He builds something steady
under your feet.

Consider This

You may not know how to answer this right now, and that's okay. Faith often starts with curiosity, not certainty.

That's exactly why this book exists.

- If you could ask God one honest question about faith, what would it be?

- When have you felt like you were trying to handle everything on your own?

- What do you hope you'll discover as you start this journey of learning who God really is and what He says about you?

Closing Prayer

Dear Lord,
Thank You for being patient with me.
For loving me even when
I've tried to do life on my own.

Teach me how to know You,
not just believe in You.
Help me to build my faith
on who You are,
not on what I can control.

When I feel unsure,
remind me that Your Word is alive
and that I can depend on You.

Let my faith grow deep,
real, and unshakable,
a steady light in every season.
Amen.

Building a Faith Foundation

The Real Struggle

Sometimes "getting close to God" feels like one more thing people say you're *supposed* to do.

Go to church.
Read the Bible.
Pray more.
Be a "good Christian."

And maybe you've thought . . .
Okay . . . but why?
What's the point?
Because honestly, life is already a lot.

School. Family. Friends. Sports. Drama.
Anxiety. Pressure. Expectations.

You're trying to keep it together,
trying to be okay,
trying to figure out who you are
and what you're doing with your life.

So, if getting close to God doesn't help
with any of that . . . why bother?
You might even think,
I don't feel anything when I pray.
Maybe God shows up for other
people, but not for me.
Maybe I've messed up too much.
Maybe this whole "God thing"
just doesn't work for me.
If you've ever felt any of that, hear this:
You're not broken.
You're not a bad person.
You're not alone.

Most people feel this way at some point.
They just don't say it out loud.

How Distance from God Actually Shows Up in Real Life

Here's something to think about:
Feeling far from God doesn't always feel like
a spiritual crisis.

Most of the time, it just feels like regular life
that quietly stops working.

It looks like this:
You feel anxious instead of peaceful.
You snap instead of staying patient.
You compare instead of celebrating.
You worry instead of trust.
You laugh with friends but feel empty afterward.

It's like trying to charge your phone
with a broken cable; everything looks normal
until you realize the battery's dying.
That slow disconnect affects everything.

It drains your peace.
It clouds your thinking.
It leaves you tired, not just physically
but emotionally and spiritually.
People say, "I'm fine."
But often, "fine" really means
"I'm barely holding it together."

Those feelings might not be random.
They might be *symptoms*,
signs that your soul is running on empty
because it's been unplugged from its
power source.

The One who gives you peace when
everything feels unsettled.
The One who gives you identity when you start
measuring yourself against everyone else.
The One who gives you strength when you're tired
of pretending you're fine.

Feeling far from God doesn't just
affect your *spiritual* life; it touches everything else.

Living Plugged In

Faith doesn't grow just because you believe in God.
It grows because you stay close to Him.

Think of it like this:
You can't charge your phone once
and expect it to last all week.
You have to keep recharging it.

The same thing happens spiritually.
A "Sunday charge" won't carry you
through a Thursday meltdown.

Connection with God isn't about perfection;
it's about rhythm.
It's in the small things:

- A quiet *Thank You* before you
  even check your phone
- One worship song while getting ready
- Choosing honesty even when
  lying would be easier
- A deep breath and *God, help me
  handle this better than I want to.*

It's not about rules.
It's about relationship.

Because the more connected you stay,
the more you start to notice His fingerprints
in ordinary moments,
a text from a friend at the perfect time,
a bit of peace that makes no sense,
a verse that lands like it was written for you.

That's how God works,
quietly, consistently,
like Wi-Fi you didn't realize was on
the whole time.

He's already present.
Already active.
Already near.

When you stop trying to do everything on your own
and begin trusting that He's with you,
something starts to shift inside.

You stop needing every situation to go your way.

You start feeling more grounded.
More calm.
More steady.

"Trust in the Lord with all your heart
and lean not on your own understanding;
in all your ways submit to him,
and he will make your paths straight."
— Proverbs 3:5–6

Maybe the secret to growing in faith
isn't trying harder at all
but letting God meet you where you already are.

When Faith Shows Up in Real Life

You know that moment when you promise yourself,
"I'm going to stay calm today,"
and then someone tests that commitment ten
minutes later?

Here's the thing:
When you stay connected to God,
you don't have to fake calmness anymore;
it starts showing up on its own.

Not instantly, but gradually, like muscle memory.

You pause before saying what you'll regret.
You notice someone who's
struggling and actually care.
You stop feeling like every disagreement is a hill to
die on.

That's real spiritual growth.
It's not about trying harder;
it's about God quietly re-wiring
what comes naturally.

> *"The fruit of the Spirit is love, joy, peace,*
> *patience, kindness, goodness, faithfulness,*
> *gentleness, and self-control."*
> *— Galatians 5:22–23 (NIV1984)*

They're not goals; they're signs that the roots of
your faith are healthy.

I used to think I had to hold everything
together, plan every detail,
fix every problem, stay strong no matter what.
But I learned that when I let go and let God lead,
things still worked out, sometimes even better.

I started to feel peace instead of pressure.
Presence instead of perfection.

Over time, His strength became my calm.
His wisdom became my pause button.
His peace became my reset.

And people noticed, not because I was perfect,
but because peace leaves fingerprints that can't
be faked.

Faith isn't about looking spiritual.
It's about finding peace where chaos used to live.

Finding Direction When You Don't Know What Comes Next

Wouldn't it be nice if God just texted you, saying,
"Here's what to do next"?

One clear message. No guessing. No confusion.

But that's not how He usually works.
He doesn't give us the whole map, just one small
step at a time.

Faith isn't a GPS; it's a relationship.

You don't get turn-by-turn directions.
You get conversation.

When you stay close to God, you start to notice
small nudges:

Wait.
Reach out.
Let that go.
Trust Me here.

Sometimes they don't make sense right away,
but that's where trust grows, in the middle of
uncertainty.

God doesn't shout over the noise.
He leads through peace.

When I feel rushed, anxious, or pressured,
it's usually *my* plan.
When I feel calm, grounded, and sure,
it's usually His.
Because God never leads with panic.

He leads with peace.

That's what faith looks like in real life:
Choosing kindness when you don't feel like it.
Walking away from drama instead of feeding it.
Praying before reacting.
Being honest when lying would be easier.
Learning that sometimes *waiting* is doing
something.

Faith isn't about having all the details.
It's about taking one small step, and then another.

Because purpose doesn't usually
appear all at once.
It grows while you walk.

You don't need to see the whole picture,
just the next step God's asking you to take.

Consider This

- Where in your life do you feel most
  "unplugged" or disconnected right now?

- What might happen if you stopped trying
  to control everything and started asking
  God for peace instead of answers?

- How could staying closer to God this week
  change how you see what's in front of you?

Closing Prayer

Dear Lord,
I'm trying to understand what faith really means,
but I'm unsure of myself as I walk this journey.

Show me how to slow down
and listen for Your voice, even when I'm uncertain.

I don't need to have everything figured out;
I just want to take small steps
and trust that You're with me.

Thank You for being patient
as I learn to grow closer to You.
Amen.

Chapter 3

The People Around You Shape the Person You Become

Who You Walk with Shapes Where You End Up

The people you spend time with
are quietly shaping you.
Their habits, words, and outlook
begin to rub off
until you can't always tell where
their influence ends and yours begins.

If your friends care about what matters,
push through the hard stuff,
and want to grow,
you'll start to catch that energy.

But when the people around you drift,
stir up drama, or shrug at bad choices,
you can get pulled into their current without
even noticing.

It's not about judging anyone.
It's about recognizing that
who you pace your life with
determines your endurance and direction.

Run beside people who challenge you
to stay the course,
not the ones who quit halfway
or distract you from the finish line.
You don't become like others
because you're weak;
you become like them
because that's how people are designed,
built for connection and influence.

Turning Up the Volume

Influence works like a volume dial.
Whatever voices you turn up the loudest
will eventually drown out the rest.
The playlists, posts, and people you listen to
most start shaping how you think, speak, and see
yourself. Ask yourself:

"Who's turned up loud in my life right now?

The friend who builds me up, or the one who tears others down?
The voice that calls out courage, or the one that keeps me afraid to try?"

Sometimes the volume gets so high you don't even notice the static; you just feel unsettled. That's when it's time to grab the dial and reset the sound.

> *"Walk with the wise and become wise, for a companion of fools suffers harm."*
> *— Proverbs 13:20*

It's not a threat; it's a reminder:
Wisdom grows in the company you keep.

Influence Is Contagious

Influence rarely announces itself.
It slips in through jokes, moods, and habits.
You start echoing the people you're around, their tone, their priorities, even their peace or frustration.

That's why God cares about your circle.
Faith isn't built only in church; it's built in car rides, text threads, and after-school hangouts where you decide what "normal" feels like.

Faith was never meant to be a solo run.

We're designed for community, but not every connection strengthens us.

When you surround yourself with people who point
you toward God, your roots grow deeper.

You begin to think differently, respond differently,
choose differently.

But if you spend most of your time in spaces
that pull you away from what's right, your faith
quietly thins, one compromise at a time.

> *"Do not be misled: 'Bad company
> corrupts good character.'"*
> *— 1 Corinthians 15:33*

Checking Your Circle

If you want a snapshot of your future, look at your
closest friends.

Do they make you stronger,
kinder, more grounded?
Or do they keep you small and distracted?

You don't need perfect friends; no one has those.
You need real ones who care about your soul, not
just your status.

People who cheer for you when you're winning
and stay when life gets messy.

Sometimes God clears space before He brings
the right people in.
That quiet season isn't punishment; it's preparation.

The Influence You Carry

Influence isn't one-sided.
You're not just soaking up energy;
you're sending it out.

People notice how you handle stress,
how you talk about others,
how you recover after making mistakes.

They notice when your peace doesn't make sense.
That's influence . . . the real kind.

So, here's a thought:
What's it like to be on the other side of you?

Do people walk away lighter or heavier?
Encouraged or exhausted?

Influence isn't about followers;
it's about leaving people better
than you found them.

Faith Friends and Everyday Friends

There's a difference between *faith friends*
and *everyday friends*, and both matter.
Faith friends remind you who
you are when you forget.
They point you back to truth
when the world gets loud.

Everyday friends might not share your faith
yet, but that doesn't make them bad.
You can still be kind, respectful, and real
without losing your direction.

Healthy love doesn't draw battle lines;
it draws boundaries.
You can care deeply for people
without copying their choices.

When Influence Turns Toxic

Sometimes a friendship drains you slowly.
It starts small—sarcasm that
stings, pressure to fit in,
invitations to things you know aren't right.

You can love people and still set limits.
Jesus did.
He spent time with everyone,
but He never let their behavior define His.

If someone's influence keeps pulling
you off track, you don't owe them an
explanation for protecting your peace.
Walking away doesn't mean you stopped caring.
It means you started growing.

A Quick Gut Check

When pressure hits, what spills out of you?
Patience or irritation?
Grace or defensiveness?

Whatever fills you will flow from you.
So ask yourself:

"What am I letting fill my
heart right now?"

If you don't like the answer, don't panic; just
start turning the dial.
Lower the noise that feeds your frustration
and raise the voices that remind you of who
you really are.

Consider This

- Who are the people you spend most of your time with?

- How do they affect your attitude, goals, or faith?

- Is there someone who helps you stay grounded and strong?

Closing Prayer

Dear Lord,
Help me see the influence I give
and receive every day.
Teach me to choose friends who build my strength
and to be that kind of friend for someone else.

When I'm tempted to follow the wrong crowd,
remind me who I'm running beside.
Let my presence bring calm,
kindness, and courage,
the kind that points others back to You.
Amen.

Chapter 4

The Truth About Love and Walking in Faith

Before we talk about dating or relationships, there's something worth saying out loud.

Not everyone is dating.
And that doesn't mean you're behind or missing something important.

Love doesn't start with another person.
It starts with God.

His love is different.
It's steady, faithful, and not dependent
on being chosen by someone else.
And it's the only kind of love that truly fulfills.

That matters, because how you understand
love shapes how you approach dating.

Let's Talk About Love

You ever notice how the word *love* gets thrown
around for almost everything?

We say we love coffee, our dog, our favorite song,
and somewhere in all that, the word kind of loses
its meaning.

But when it comes to dating, love
feels a lot more personal.
It's exciting, unpredictable, and
sometimes confusing.

It can make you feel seen and wanted one
minute and completely unsure the next.
When you're dating, it can feel
like love, and in a way, it is.

It's friendship, chemistry, connection.
But it's not the forever kind of love God designed
for marriage, the kind built on promise, patience,
and trust.

Dating love is where you learn about yourself,
about others, and about what you value.
Real love, the kind that lasts, shows up
with respect, honesty, and self-control.

Knowing What You Want
Before You Get There

It's a lot easier to say what you believe
before you're caught up in the moment.
Because once emotions take over,
it's hard to think clearly.

Your heart races, logic fades, and the only thing
that seems real is what's happening right then.
That's why it's important to think ahead, even when
you're just casually dating.

Ask yourself:

"What do I really want from this relationship?
What do I want to give?
How far am I willing to go before I lose something I
can't get back?"

You can't make those decisions in the heat
of passion; your thoughts don't work the
same when feelings are running the show.
That's why wisdom matters before emotion.

When Things Get Real

This is probably one of the most life-shaping
moments you'll face so far, the kind that quietly
molds who you're becoming, whether you realize it
or not.

It's defining because what you decide in this
space, between what feels good now and what's
truly right for you, reveals what you value most.
It shows how much you believe your
future is worth protecting.

And it becomes a part of your story that either
strengthens your faith or leaves you wondering
how you lost your way.

No one plans to lose themselves in a relationship.
It just happens, one small compromise
at a time, until you're left wondering
how something that started out feeling
so right ended up feeling so heavy.

That's why this moment matters.
Because the decisions you make in love
aren't just about feelings; they shape
your heart, your confidence, your boundaries,
and the kind of person you're becoming.

Safe Sex Isn't the Whole Story

When people talk about "safe sex," they
usually mean birth control or condoms.
But that's not the kind of safety
God is talking about.

Real safety guards more than your body; it shields
your heart, your peace, your future, and your faith.

God designed sex to come after marriage,

not to take away your freedom,
but to protect your heart.

Because when you give your body to someone,
you give them part of your heart too.
And when that relationship ends, and most teenage
ones do, those pieces don't fit back perfectly.

God isn't trying to control you.
He's trying to protect you.

He knows what heartbreak feels like,
and He wants to save you from carrying
pain you were never meant to hold.
That's not control; that's love.

Getting Lost in the Moment May Take Decades to Recover From

There's a reason people say,
"Think before you act."
Because sometimes one moment,
one decision, can echo for years.

Attraction love sounds like this:

"I need you."
"I want you."
"I can't stop, just this one time."
"No one will ever know."

It feels powerful, like the whole world
disappears and it's just the two of you.
Your heart is racing, your thoughts blur, and in that
moment, it feels impossible to pull away.

That's what attraction does;
it's strong, emotional, and real.
But attraction love is about *now*.
It wants what feels right in the moment, not what's
best for tomorrow.

Respectful love sounds like this:

"Let's slow down; we need to stop."
"I don't want to put you in a position
to disappoint your parents."
"I want to protect your future plans and mine."
"I care about your reputation and mine."

Respectful love still feels the emotion,
but it listens to wisdom.
It doesn't shut down passion; it just refuses to let
passion take over.

It says, "I care about you too much to let this be the
moment that rewrites our story."

And here's something not many people say
out loud: Too often, one person assumes
the other will be the strong one.
They wait for someone else to set the boundary,
to say, "Stop," to take control.

But that's putting your future in
someone else's hands.
Real maturity means being the one who steps up.

Because if you're both waiting for the other person
to take control, it's already too late.

While attraction love often centers on the
immediate desire for physical connection, true love
embodies a deeper commitment, where protection,
understanding, and respect form the foundation of
a lasting bond.

It's real love guided by purpose, not pressure,
the kind of love God designed, one that honors,
protects, and waits.

My great-aunt used to say,
"Puppy love leads to a dog's life."

I laughed when I was younger, but she was right.
If you chase every feeling without wisdom, you can
lose sight of who you are, and it can take years to
find your way back.

Getting lost in the moment can take
decades to recover from.
And that's what no one tells you—how long regret
can echo.

How one small yes in a moment of pressure can
follow you into seasons you never meant to carry it.

Love Guided by Guardrails

When you're learning to drive, one of the first
things you notice on the road is the guardrails.
They don't move. They don't bend. They just stand
there, quietly keeping you safe.

At first, they seem unnecessary.
You might even think, *Why do they have to line the
road like that? I can see just fine.*

But when you hit a curve, drive through the
mountains, or feel your tires slide on wet pavement,
suddenly those guardrails make sense.

They're not there to block your freedom;
they're there to protect your life.

Love works the same way.

The boundaries God sets aren't meant
to limit you; they're meant to keep
you from going over the edge.
They keep your story on the road, your heart intact,
and your future within reach.

Because love without boundaries is like
speeding near a cliff with no guardrail;
it feels thrilling until you realize there's
nothing left to stop you from falling.

So when God says, "Wait," "Not yet," or "This is
sacred," He's not trying to take away your fun;
He's trying to protect your destination.

Real love doesn't need to test the limits.
It knows the journey's worth finishing well.

For Those Who've Been
Hurt or Pressured

Not everyone chooses what happens to them.
Some people have moments taken from them
through pressure, manipulation, or force.

If that's part of your story, please
hear this: It's not your fault.
You didn't ruin your future.
You didn't lose your worth.

What someone else did to you does not define who
you are.

God's grace covers what was done to you
just as much as what you've done.
You can start from a clean slate,
right here, right now.

You don't have to stay trapped in shame or silence.
God can bring healing, peace, and even purpose
out of pain.

You are still loved.
You are still whole.
And your story isn't over.

And if you've made decisions you regret,
if you crossed lines, gave in to pressure,

or had moments where your judgment
slipped, you can still start fresh.

God's grace doesn't run out when you mess up.
It meets you right where you are and gives you the
strength to begin again.

You don't have to carry guilt or shame.
You can hand it to God, learn from it, and walk
forward knowing you're forgiven and loved.

He's not done writing your story, and the next
chapter can be one of healing, peace, and wisdom.

*"Love each other with genuine affection,
and take delight in honoring each other."*
— Romans 12:10 (NLT)

That verse isn't about rules; it's about honor.
Real love honors before it touches.
It stops when it should.
It protects even when it's hard.
And it listens to the voice of God
over the voice of emotion.

A Word to the Girls

You don't have to be all that or be the most
popular person in the room to be noticed.
Real beauty isn't about attention;
it's about authenticity.

It's easy to feel pressure to look
perfect, act confident, and always
seem like you have it all together.
Social media tells you that being desirable is the
same as being valued, but that's a lie.

You are already loved, fully, completely,
and without needing to earn it.
God's love doesn't depend on how many people
notice you or how many likes you get.

But here's something important:
You have more influence than you think.
What feels harmless—a flirt, a joke, a glance—
can send messages you never meant to send.
What seems like fun can quickly turn confusing,
especially when emotions get involved.

It's easy to test boundaries, to tease, to see
how far someone might go, but be careful.
What starts as curiosity can become pressure,
on you and on someone else.

Confidence and kindness never have to compete.

You can be strong without being harsh,
noticed without being reckless,
and bold without losing your peace.

When you love yourself the way God loves you,
you'll attract the kind of people who see your
value too, not because of your looks or charm, but
because of your heart.

So before you send that message or
chase attention that fades, pause.
You don't need to prove you're
desirable; you already are.
Save your heart for someone who's ready to honor
it, not just hold it.

Because this isn't just about love.
It's about who you're becoming
and the kind of woman God is shaping you to be.

A Word to the Guys

There's a lot of noise today about
what it means to be a man.
Some say it's about being tough,
being popular, or always having the last word.
But that kind of manhood is shallow; it fades fast.

Real strength looks different.
It's not loud or flashy.
It's steady.
It's choosing to protect, not pressure.
To lead with integrity, not ego.

A friend once told me about his dad,
a God-fearing, God-loving farmer
through and through.
One day, in a quiet conversation
with his grandson, the boy asked him,
"Grandpa, what made you be you?"

The old man smiled and said,
**"When I was eighteen years old, I decided to be
a good man."**

That's it. No speeches, no titles, just a choice.
Because being a good man doesn't
happen by accident.
It's a decision, one you make over and over again,
even when it's hard.

One path leads to confusion,
broken trust, hurt hearts, and regret.

The other builds something lasting,
peace, confidence, and respect.

So here's the challenge:
Be that guy, the one who protects,
respects, and leads with integrity.
The one who listens to God
when emotions are loud.
The one who values honor over
ego and truth over attention.

Because this isn't just about love.
It's about who you're becoming
and the kind of man God is shaping you to be.

Consider This

- Can you tell the difference between attraction and real love?

- What does it look like to honor someone you care about, not just in words, but in how you treat them?

- When emotions run high, who do you trust to remind you of your worth?

- How do you define respectful love in your own life?

Closing Prayer

Dear Lord,
You know my heart, the parts that want
to be loved, to be seen, to belong.
Teach me what real love looks like, the kind that
honors You and protects what matters most.

When emotions get loud, help me remember that
waiting isn't weakness; it's wisdom.

Give me the courage to set boundaries,
to speak up, and to walk away when I need to.

Let my choices in love bring peace, not pressure,
and remind me that I am already loved by You.
Amen.

Chapter 5

You Were Born on Purpose

Born for a Reason

You might not think about it much, but the fact that you're even *here*, breathing, reading this, living in this exact moment in history, isn't random.

It's easy to believe life just *happens*. School, friends, social media, goals—they all blend into one long scroll of ordinary days. But underneath it all, there's purpose.

You were born on purpose, for a reason that reaches beyond what you see right now. God designed you with intention, not accident. He wired your personality, your gifts, even your quirks, to fit into His bigger picture.

You might not have it all figured out yet;
that's okay.
Purpose doesn't show up all at once like a
flash of lightning.
It grows slowly as you learn to trust the One who
made you.

And here's the thing: God didn't wait until
you were perfect before He called you.
He chose you because He already
sees who you can become.
Even the parts of your story that feel ordinary or
messy, those are pieces He can still use.

When God created you, He looked at your life,
every year, every experience, every detail . . .
and said, "That one's Mine. I've got plans for them."
Not generic plans, not copy-and-paste dreams,
but something unique.

Your life matters because your
Creator decided it would.
You're not a filler person in someone else's story.
You have an important place in the
story God is still writing.

You don't have to chase your purpose;
it's already woven into who you are.
God's design wasn't rushed or random. It was
thoughtful, personal, and full of potential.

> *"For we are God's masterpiece.*
> *He has created us anew in Christ*

> *Jesus, so we can do the good things*
> *He planned for us long ago."*
> *— Ephesians 2:10 (NLT)*

That means your life isn't an
accident or an afterthought.
You were imagined by God, shaped with
purpose, and placed in this time for a reason.

The Designer Knows the Design

When someone designs something,
a phone, a car, a piece of art, they know
exactly how it's meant to work.
The same is true for you.

God designed you, which means He knows what
helps you thrive . . . and what pulls you off track.

You don't have to guess who you're meant to be.
The One who made you already knows, and He's
more interested in showing you *how* to live than
leaving you to figure it out on your own.

That's why time with God matters so much.
You can't expect to live in your purpose
without knowing the One who designed it.
It's like trying to play a game without
understanding the rules; you'll move a lot,
never in the right direction.

Living out God's design doesn't mean having
your life mapped out by age eighteen.
It means asking, "What has God already given me,
and how can I use it right where I am?"

Your gifts, your personality, your way of
caring for people, those aren't random.
They're clues to your calling.
And every day you choose kindness
instead of judgment, faith instead of fear,
and honesty instead of pressure, you're
living out what you were made for.

God isn't waiting for you to be older,
smarter, or more experienced.
He's ready to use you now, in your school, your
family, your friend group, and your community.

When you walk in step with the Designer, life
starts to make sense in ways it never did before.
You begin to see how all the pieces, even the hard
ones, fit into something bigger.

> *"You created my inmost being;*
> *you knit me together in my mother's womb.*
> *I praise you because I am fearfully*
> *and wonderfully made."*
> *— Psalm 139:13–14*

God knows your design because
He's the One who shaped it.
And when you trust the Designer, you don't
have to force purpose to happen; you just have
to walk with Him daily and let it unfold.

Purpose Isn't a Job; It's a Journey

When people talk about purpose, it's easy to
picture some big, dramatic moment, like God
dropping a plan from the sky with your name on it.
But that's not usually how it works.

Purpose isn't a job title.
It's not your college major, or your career
choice, or your five-year plan.
Purpose is who you're becoming as you walk with
God and how your life reflects His love.

It's built in the small, steady moments,
the ones no one else sees.
When you show up for a friend who's hurting.
When you forgive someone who doesn't deserve it.
When you use your voice to encourage
instead of tear down.
That's purpose in action.

You don't need to wait until you have your "dream
life" to live like your life matters; it already does.
God doesn't measure your worth
by success or popularity.
He measures it by faithfulness, by what you do with
what He's already given you.

Every time you choose what's right
when it would've been easier not to,
you're walking in purpose.

Every time you pray, listen, or obey that small
nudge in your heart, you're walking in purpose.
Every time you decide to live differently,
even when no one else understands,
you're walking in purpose.

Your calling isn't one big moment;
it's a lifetime of small ones.
It's a journey of growing, trusting, and becoming.

Like a Lighthouse in the Fog

Think of purpose like a lighthouse on a foggy night.
You might not see every detail of the
shoreline, but you can still see the light.
It doesn't flash a map of every turn ahead; it simply
shows enough for the next few steps.

When you keep your eyes on that light,
God's truth, His Word, His steady presence,
you won't drift off course, even when
everything around you feels uncertain.
The fog might hide your destination for a while, but
the light never moves.

Purpose works the same way.
God doesn't hand you the entire plan because
He's teaching you to trust the light, not the view.
You don't have to see the whole path to know
you're being guided.

Each act of obedience is another
step toward clarity.
Each small yes brings you closer to
what He's preparing you for.
The journey might feel slow, but
the light never stops shining.

How God Reveals Purpose

God doesn't hide your purpose like it's some
secret treasure you have to chase down.
He reveals it slowly, intentionally, and often through
ordinary moments.

Sometimes He uses your gifts . . . the things that
come naturally to you, encouraging, creating,
organizing, helping. They're hints of what you were
made to do.

Sometimes He uses people . . . a teacher
who believes in you, a friend who sees
something good that you didn't, even a
person who challenges you. God uses all
kinds of voices to shape your direction.

And sometimes, He uses hard seasons . . .
heartbreak, disappointment, failure. Those
are often where purpose grows deepest.
Because when you have to rely on God to keep
going, He teaches you things about yourself you'd
never learn any other way.

You don't have to understand it all right now.
You just have to stay close enough
to hear Him when He speaks.
That's how purpose unfolds, not in one big reveal,
but through a hundred small whispers.

The more you walk with Him, the more you
recognize His voice in the everyday—a thought that
sticks, a verse that hits differently, a conversation
that feels like confirmation.

> *"And we know that in all things God works*
> *for the good of those who love him, who*
> *have been called according to his purpose."*
> *— Romans 8:28*

When You Feel Lost or Unqualified

Let's be honest; some days you don't feel
like you're walking on purpose at all.
You feel behind, unsure, or like everyone else
already got their plan and you somehow missed
the memo.

Maybe you've made mistakes that make
you question if God could still use you.
Or maybe you just don't feel spiritual enough to do
anything that really matters.

But here's the truth: God's plan has always started
with imperfect people who said yes.

Moses doubted himself. David messed up.
Esther was terrified. Paul fought against the faith
he later preached.
And yet God used every one of them, not because
they were perfect, but because they were willing.

Purpose isn't about being flawless;
it's about being available.
It's saying, "God, I don't feel ready,
but I trust You anyway."

So, when you feel lost, remember that being
uncertain doesn't mean you're off track. Sometimes
it's proof you're learning to depend on Him instead
of yourself.

> *"My grace is all you need. My power*
> *works best in weakness."*
> *— 2 Corinthians 12:9 (NLT)*

Living It Out Daily

You don't have to wait for a big "God moment"
to start walking in your purpose; it's already
happening, right here, in your everyday life.

Purpose isn't something that starts later.
It's the way you live now, how you treat people
when no one's watching, the words you choose

online, how you respond when you're left out or tempted to tear someone down.

That's walking in purpose.

It's not flashy, but it's powerful, because you're showing the world what God looks like through your actions.

When you forgive someone instead of
holding a grudge, that's purpose.
When you help your younger sibling
without being asked, that's purpose.
When you pray for a friend instead of
gossiping about them, that's purpose.
When you speak up for what's right, even if your
voice shakes, that's purpose.

Purpose isn't about doing more; it's about living aware, recognizing that God's with you in every hallway, every conversation, every decision.

And when you mess up—because you will—you don't start over from zero. You just keep walking. God's not keeping score; He's shaping your heart.

> *"Whatever you do, do it all*
> *for the glory of God."*
> *— 1 Corinthians 10:31*

That verse isn't about doing big religious things. It's about doing everything, even the small, everyday stuff, in a way that honors God.

When you live that way, even the most ordinary day becomes something sacred.

Consider This

- What if the very things you've been overlooking, your gifts, your struggles, your everyday moments, are the way God is showing you what you're made for?

- How might trusting God's design change the way you see your own potential today?

- What if the very thing you think disqualifies you is actually what God wants to use most?

Closing Prayer

Dear Lord,
Thank You for creating me on purpose, for giving
me gifts, dreams, and a reason to be here.
Help me see my life the way You see it, not as
random or ordinary, but as something that matters.

When I start to doubt who I am or where I'm
going, remind me that You're still writing my
story. Show me how to live out my purpose in
the small things, at school, with friends, at home,
so that everything I do points back to You.

When I don't know the next step,
help me trust that You do.
And when I get it wrong, help me
remember that You never walk away;
You simply invite me to start again.

Thank You for making me fearfully and wonderfully,
for giving me a life that has meaning, and for
loving me enough to lead me through it.
Amen.

Chapter 6

Why Does God Let Bad Things Happen?

Sometimes life just doesn't make sense.
A tragedy hits the news.
Someone you love gets sick.
You lose someone too soon.
And you wonder, "If God is good, why would He let this happen?"

You're not the first to ask that.
Even the strongest people in the Bible
wrestled with the same question.

Joseph's Story—When Life Falls Apart

You may have heard of *Joseph and the Amazing Technicolor Dreamcoat*, the musical, the movie, or maybe just the name.

But before it ever became a Broadway story, it was a real one, told in **Genesis 37–50**.

Joseph was his father's favorite.
His dad, Jacob, made it obvious; he
gave Joseph a bright, colorful coat that
practically shouted, "You're special!"
That coat wasn't just a fashion
statement; it was a symbol of favor.
And his brothers noticed.
Jealousy turned to bitterness, and bitterness turned
to betrayal.

Then came the dreams.
Joseph told his brothers about the visions God had
given him, that one day he'd stand in a position
of leadership, and they'd bow before him.
He didn't mean it arrogantly; he just believed
God was showing him something.
But his brothers didn't see it that way.

One day, jealousy went too far.
Joseph's brothers threw him into a pit and
sold him to traders heading for Egypt.
He went from being the favorite son to being a
slave in a foreign land.

If you've ever felt forgotten, betrayed, or stuck in a
situation that didn't make sense, Joseph gets it.
But what looked like an ending was actually the
beginning of something incredible.

In Egypt, Joseph was falsely accused and
thrown into prison, again unfairly.
Yet even there, he didn't stop trusting God.

He used his gift of interpreting
dreams to help others.
Years later, that gift opened a door straight
to Pharaoh, the ruler of Egypt.
Joseph went from prisoner to second-in-command
of the entire nation.

And when famine hit the land, the same brothers
who sold him showed up begging for food,
not realizing the man in charge was Joseph.
He could have chosen revenge.
Instead, he chose forgiveness.

He told them, "You meant it to harm me, but
God used it for good" (see **Genesis 50:20**).
That's not denial; that's redemption.
Joseph saw that what others meant for evil, God
had turned into something that saved lives.

Why Bad Things Happen

The truth is, the world wasn't always this way.
When God first created it, everything
was good, no pain, no fear, no loss.
People lived in perfect peace with each other and
with God.

Then came a choice.
Adam and Eve decided to go their own
way instead of trusting God's.
It wasn't just about eating fruit;
it was about thinking they knew better.

That moment cracked the world.
It let pain, selfishness, sickness, and death into a
story that had once been perfect.

God didn't cause the brokenness;
human choices did.
And every generation since has
felt the ripple effects.

So, when bad things happen, when there's
injustice, illness, tragedy, or heartbreak,
it's not because God stopped caring.
It's because the world itself is still broken.

But here's the hope: God never left.
He stepped right into the mess through Jesus.
He came to show us what love looks like in a
hurting world and to promise that one day, all the
pain will be made right.

We may never understand *why*
every hard thing happens,
but we can know *who* walks through it with us.

Beauty in the Broken

Have you ever heard of the
Japanese art of *kintsugi*?
It's the practice of taking broken
pottery and repairing it with gold.

The cracks aren't hidden; they're highlighted.
The once-shattered piece becomes stronger and
more valuable because of what it's been through.

That's what God does with our brokenness.
He doesn't erase it; He restores it.
The scars become the places where His grace
shines through.

Maybe you've faced something that cracked you:
grief, trauma, betrayal, fear.
God doesn't expect you to pretend it didn't hurt.

He just wants you to hand Him the pieces.
Because in His hands, what was broken can
become something beautiful.

> *"The Lord will fight for you;*
> *you need only to be still."*
> *— Exodus 14:14*

Consider This

- When life doesn't make sense, do you tend to pull closer to God or push away?

- Can you think of a time when something painful eventually led to something good?

- What "broken piece" of your story do you need to hand over to God today?

Closing Prayer

Dear Lord,
Sometimes the world feels so heavy, full of things I
don't understand.

Remind me that You see what I can't.
When life feels unfair, help me trust that You're still
working behind the scenes.

Show me how to find purpose in the
pain, peace in the waiting,
and beauty in the broken places of my life.
Amen.

Chapter 7

Rebuilding My Life with God

When Everything Feels Like It's Falling Apart

There are seasons when life just feels heavy.
Home doesn't feel peaceful; maybe
there's tension, change, or distance.
Friendships shift.
People you thought would always
be there start to drift.
School pressure builds, grades drop,
or anxiety creeps in.
Sometimes you face things no one your age should
have to handle: bullying, betrayal, heartbreak, loss,
or feeling completely unseen.

And you wonder, "Why does it feel like God is
distant when I need Him the most?"

Sometimes it's not one big thing; it's a lot
of little things that finally make you feel
like you can't hold it together anymore.
You still smile, still post, still show up, but inside,
you're tired.

That's when rebuilding begins, not because
you suddenly feel strong, but because you
finally realize you can't do it alone.

What Grace Really Means

You've heard the word *grace* before, but
maybe you've never really understood it.
Grace is God giving you what you don't deserve:
His love, forgiveness, and a chance to start again,
even after you've messed up.

It's not about earning His favor
or proving your worth.
Grace means that no matter what happened,
God's love hasn't changed.

Grace says, "You don't have to be perfect. You just
have to come."

The Bible is full of people who messed
up big but still found grace.
Peter denied even knowing Jesus.

David made choices that hurt people deeply.
Jonah ran the opposite direction
when God called him.

They all failed, and yet God still loved them, forgave
them, and used their stories to help others.

*"But God demonstrates his own
love for us in this: While we were
still sinners, Christ died for us."*
— Romans 5:8

Grace means you don't have to work
harder to make God love you.
You don't have to earn your way back to Him
because you never lost His love to begin with.

*"For it is by grace you have been saved,
through faith—and this is not from
yourselves, it is the gift of God—not by
works, so that no one can boast."*
— Ephesians 2:8–9

Grace isn't just about getting a second chance;
it's about what Jesus already did for you.

When He died on the cross, He took
the weight of every sin, every mistake,
every regret, so you could be free.
That's how you get to heaven.
You heard me correctly:
That's how you get to heaven.
That's the only way to heaven.

You can't earn your way in, buy your way in,
or be "good enough" to deserve it.
It's only through faith in what Jesus did, believing
He died for you and rose again and accepting His
forgiveness as your own.

It's as simple as saying,
"Jesus, I believe You died for me.
I believe You rose again. I accept Your
forgiveness and want to follow You."

That moment, your acknowledgment of what He
did, opens the door to eternal life and starts a new
chapter of walking with Him.

Think of it as a road trip.
You can have a car full of gas, snacks, and good
music, but you'll never reach your destination if you
don't know where you're going. And you can't get
there without directions.

Grace is both.
It's your destination . . . heaven . . . and
it's also your roadmap, Jesus.
He shows you the way home, one turn at a time.

Grace doesn't erase the past.
It rewrites your future.
Grace says, "What happened before doesn't
have to define what comes next."

Rebuilding Starts Small

When you start rebuilding your life with
God, it doesn't happen overnight.
It's small steps, simple, steady, everyday choices
that slowly shape something new.

It looks like this:

- Opening your Bible even when
  you don't know where to start
- Praying honestly, not perfectly
- Listening to worship music instead
  of letting your mind spiral
- Filling your heart with faith-based
  podcasts and messages that speak
  about life instead of noise
- Choosing time with God
  over endless scrolling

These are bricks of trust, one on top of another,
forming a stronger foundation than before.

You're not earning your way back;
you're reconnecting to the One who never left.

When You Feel Like Giving Up

There will still be moments when you fall
apart again, when you doubt, mess up, or
question if this faith thing is even working.
But remember this promise:

> *"The Lord will fight for you;*
> *you need only to be still."*
> *— Exodus 14:14*

God isn't asking you to fix everything; He's
inviting you to rest while He fights for you.
Through Jesus, heaven wasn't kept far away.
God brought His presence close,
and through the Holy Spirit,
He's with you even now.
He rebuilds what feels broken, restores
what feels lost, and turns even the hardest
seasons into something meaningful.

Consider This

- What areas of your life need rebuilding right now?

- Where have you been trying to hold things together on your own?

- How could you invite God into those spaces today?

- What "road trip directions" might you be ignoring because you think you already know the way?

Closing Prayer

Dear Lord,
Thank You for loving me even when I've tried to do
life on my own.

Teach me what it means to rebuild with You,
to trust You more and depend on You daily.
Help me to remember that grace is enough, that I
don't have to earn Your love.

When I start to drift, pull me back.
Show me how to grow stronger through prayer,
Scripture, and time with You.

And when I feel lost, remind me that You're
still guiding every step of the way.
Amen.

Chapter 8

Forgiveness: Letting Go and Letting God Heal

When Forgiveness Feels Impossible

Forgiveness might be one of the
hardest things you'll ever do.
Letting go of hurt can feel like letting someone
"off the hook," and that doesn't seem fair.

Maybe you've tried to forgive, but the
pain keeps replaying in your mind.
You think about what they said, what they did,
what they *should* have done differently.
You replay the moment,
trying to rewrite it in your head.

Forgiveness isn't easy.

For many people, it's one of the last things
they're willing to hand over to God.
It takes time, prayer, and a lot of faith.

A friend once asked,
"Would you rather be right . . . or have peace?"

That question lingers because when you hold on to
anger, you're choosing to stay tied to the very thing
that hurts you.

Forgiveness isn't pretending it didn't happen.
It's deciding not to let what happened
define you anymore.

What Forgiveness Really Means

The world says you have a right to stay angry.
People tell you, "You don't owe them forgiveness."
And honestly, that feels good for a while.
It feels powerful. It feels safe.

But eventually, that kind of power
starts to feel heavy.
You carry it everywhere, in your words,
your thoughts, your sleep.
It becomes a weight you were never meant to carry.

That's why God talks so much about forgiveness,
not because He wants you to excuse what
happened, but because He doesn't want bitterness
to control your heart.

> *"Get rid of all bitterness, rage and anger. . . . Be kind and compassionate to one another, forgiving each other, just as in Christ God forgave you."*
> *— Ephesians 4:31–32*

Forgiveness doesn't mean you
trust that person again.
It doesn't mean what they did was okay.
It means you're giving the situation to God,
letting Him carry the justice and the healing.

When you forgive, it's no longer
between you and them.
It's between *them and God.*

You've done your part.
You've chosen peace.
Now God handles the rest.

Why It's So Hard

Forgiveness is hard because it goes against
everything in our human nature.
We want things to feel fair.
We want people to apologize first.
We want proof that they've changed.

But forgiveness isn't a transaction;
it's an act of trust.

It's saying, "God, I'm releasing this to You because I
can't carry it anymore."

And sometimes it's not a one-time thing.
It's daily, maybe even hourly.
Each time the memory rises, you remind yourself,
"I've already given that to God."

That's what healing looks like,
not forgetting, but releasing.

> *"Bear with each other and forgive one*
> *another if any of you has a grievance. . . .*
> *Forgive as the Lord forgave you."*
> *— Colossians 3:13*

The Weight You Were
Never Meant to Carry

Picture walking through life with a heavy backpack.
Every time someone hurts you,
another stone gets dropped in.
At first, you think, *It's fine; I can handle this.*
But over time, it gets heavier.
You start to slow down, your shoulders ache, and
even small things feel hard to carry.

That's what unforgiveness does.
It wears you down.
It steals your peace.

But when you choose to forgive, even
when you don't *feel* it, it's like setting that
backpack down for the first time.
You can finally breathe again.

Opening Your Hand

When you hold on to anger or pain, it's like
clenching your fist as tightly as you can.
At first, it feels strong, like you're in control.
But after a while, your hand starts to hurt.
You realize the strength it takes to hold on is
actually draining you.

Forgiveness is the moment you open your hand.
You release what you were never meant to keep.
And when you finally let go, God can fill that empty
space with peace.

That's the quiet power of forgiveness;
it creates room for God to heal what
you couldn't fix on your own.

Where Faith Becomes Real

Forgiveness is often where faith stops
being an idea and starts becoming real.
It's where you move from knowing *about* God's
grace to actually *experiencing* it.

You begin to see that faith isn't just
believing He exists; it's trusting Him
enough to handle what broke you.
It's the moment your faith takes root and starts to
transform the way you think, respond, and love.

> *"If you forgive other people when*
> *they sin against you, your heavenly*
> *Father will also forgive you."*
> *— Matthew 6:14*

Forgiveness is freedom.
It's the doorway God uses to bring healing,
peace, and even unexpected joy.
It's not easy, but it's worth everything it costs.

How to Begin Letting Go

You don't have to figure it out all at once.
Start small.

Talk to God honestly. Tell Him who hurt you and
how it still affects you.

Ask for help. You can't forgive on your own, and
you don't have to.

Pray for peace more than payback. God can handle
justice better than we ever could.

Release control. Forgiveness doesn't erase what
happened, but it frees your heart to heal.

Forgiveness is a process.
Sometimes you'll feel like you've moved on; then
one memory hits and you're back in the pain again.

That's okay. Healing isn't linear.
Just keep giving it back to God, over and over if you
have to.

He's patient.
He understands.
And every time you release it, your
peace grows stronger.

Consider This

- Have you ever said you forgave
  someone but still felt angry inside?
  What made it hard to actually let go?

- When someone hurts you, what's your first
  reaction: shut down, fight back, or hold it in?

- What do you think would happen if
  you asked God to help you forgive,
  even if you didn't "feel" ready yet?

- Can you imagine what kind of peace you
  might feel if you stopped replaying what
  happened and started releasing it to God?

Closing Prayer

Dear Lord,
You know the pain I've been holding, the words, the
actions, the moments that broke my heart.

I don't want to carry it anymore.

Teach me how to forgive, even
when it feels impossible.
Help me to release my anger, my hurt, and my
need to be right. Replace it with Your peace.

Thank You for forgiving me over and over
again. It's a gift I could never earn.
Heal what's broken in me and use it for
something good. Let Your grace fill the empty
spaces where bitterness used to live.
Amen.

Chapter 9

Learning to Pray and Hearing God's Voice

When Talking to God Feels Awkward

Prayer can feel weird at first, like you're talking to
the air or sending messages that don't get read.
You start wondering if you're doing
it wrong, if you're saying the right
words, or if God even hears you.

But prayer isn't a speech; it's a conversation.
You don't have to sound "churchy."
You don't even have to close your eyes or fold your
hands (though you can).

God just wants to hear your voice,
your real, unfiltered thoughts.
The questions, the worries, the random
things you think don't matter—they do.

Because prayer isn't about perfection;
it's about connection.

What Prayer Really Is

Think of prayer like texting your closest friend.
Sometimes you send a long message
that pours everything out.
Other times it's just a quick,
"Hey, I need you right now."

And even when you don't get a reply right away,
you still know the message was received.

That's what prayer is like with God.
He's always connected. Always listening.
Sometimes He answers through a verse you
read, a sudden sense of peace, or a person
who says exactly what you needed to hear.
Other times He's silent, not because He doesn't
care, but because He's working behind the scenes.

How to Pray (Without Overthinking It)

If you're not sure where to start, Jesus already gave
us a model.

It's called the Lord's Prayer.
It's not meant to be memorized word-for-word, but
to show what prayer looks like:

> *"Our Father in heaven,*
> *hallowed be your name,*
> *your kingdom come,*
> *your will be done,*
> *on earth as it is in heaven.*
> *Give us today our daily bread.*
> *And forgive us our debts,*
> *as we also have forgiven our debtors.*
> *And lead us not into temptation,*
> *but deliver us from the evil one."*
> *— Matthew 6:9–13*

Let's break that down:

- **"Our Father in heaven"** — You're talking to someone who loves you deeply.
- **"Your kingdom come, your will be done"** — You're trusting God's plan more than your own.
- **"Give us today our daily bread"** — You can ask for what you need each day.
- **"Forgive us our debts, as we also have forgiven our debtors"** — You're being honest about where you've messed up while also forgiving others so you don't stay stuck in bitterness.
- **"Lead us not into temptation, but deliver us from the evil one"** — You're asking God to help you make strong choices when life tries to pull you off-track.

That's prayer: simple, honest, real.

Prayer in Real Life

Here's the thing: You can talk
to God about *anything.*
Yes, even your math test.
Even your team's big game.

You can absolutely pray for your
grades and your sports teams!
Prayer isn't limited to "serious" things;
it's about sharing what matters to you.

When you pray about your grades, you're not
asking God to magically give you the answers.
You're asking Him to give you focus, confidence,
and peace when you study and take that test.
You're saying, "God, help me to do my best and
trust You with the outcome."

And when you pray for your team,
you're not just asking to win.
You're asking for safety, teamwork,
encouragement, and the ability to play
with integrity, no matter what happens.

That's what makes prayer powerful:
It invites God into the middle of
your *everyday moments.*
Whether it's classes, practice, friendships,
or fears, God wants to be part of it all.

How God Speaks Back

Sometimes people expect to hear God's
voice like a loud, dramatic movie moment:
thunder, angels, or writing in the sky.
But usually, it's quiet.

You might notice things:

- A verse that keeps coming up
- A peace you can't explain
- A thought that feels like wisdom, not fear
- A "coincidence" that's too
  perfect to be random

That's often how God speaks.
He guides through peace, not pressure.

> *"My sheep listen to my voice; I know*
> *them, and they follow me."*
> *— John 10:27*

When Jesus said this, He was describing how close
He wants to be to us, like a shepherd who knows
every one of His sheep by name.

The more time you spend with Him, the easier it is
to recognize His voice, not as an audible sound, but
as a quiet nudge that brings peace instead of panic.

When You Don't Hear Anything

Sometimes it feels like God's not responding at all, like your prayers are just floating in space. But silence doesn't mean absence.

Think of it like sending a text that says, "Delivered." You don't see a typing bubble yet, but you know the message went through.

That's what prayer is like.
You may not see the typing bubble, but God's already working.

> *"In repentance and rest is your salvation, in quietness and trust is your strength."*
> *— Isaiah 30:15*

Sometimes the strongest thing you can do is stop striving and let God carry the weight.

He might not answer in the way or timing you expect, but His silence is never rejection; it's usually preparation.

Consider This

- What kinds of things do you usually talk to God about, and what do you avoid bringing up?

- When you pray, do you ever feel like you're just "checking a box"? What might change if you saw it as an actual conversation?

- What helps you feel close to God—music, journaling, being outside, reading Scripture? Try starting there when you pray.

- If prayer is your text to God, what's one thing you'd say to Him right now, no filters, no perfect words?

Closing Prayer

Dear Lord,
Sometimes I don't know what to say,
and sometimes I'm not even sure You're listening.
But I want to talk to You, really talk.

Teach me how to hear You in the quiet,
how to notice You in my day,
and how to trust that You're working even when I
can't see it.

Let my prayers be honest, not perfect.
Thank You for always being there,
even in the silence.
Amen.

Chapter 10

Living Differently in a World That's Lost Its Way

When the World Feels Like It's Spinning

It's easy to feel overwhelmed by
what's happening around you.
Social media makes everyone's
highlight reel look perfect.
Friends change opinions overnight.
Right and wrong start to blur.
You scroll and think, *How do I even fit in here?*

The truth is, the world drifts.
It changes with every new trend,
every new opinion, every wave of pressure.
But faith gives you something the
world can't: an anchor.

Anchored, Not Drifting

Imagine standing on a boat in
the middle of the ocean.
If you don't drop an anchor, the current
will pull you wherever it wants.
You might not even notice at first, just a slow drift
until land disappears behind you.

That's what happens spiritually when
we stop staying close to God.
We start drifting with whatever
feels right in the moment,
the crowd's opinion, the newest trend,
the loudest voice.
But when your anchor is faith, you can stay steady
even when the current shifts.

> *"We have this hope as an anchor*
> *for the soul, firm and secure."*
> *— Hebrews 6:19*

Your relationship with God is that anchor.
It keeps you grounded when life feels
uncertain and reminds you who you are
when the world tries to tell you otherwise.

When You Feel the Pull

The world will pull at you in quiet ways:

- Pressure to fit in, even when it means compromising your values
- The need for likes and approval
- Temptations to hide your faith so you don't stand out
- Messages that say, "Do whatever makes you happy," even if it hurts someone else

Drifting doesn't always look like rebellion;
sometimes it just looks like distraction.
But every choice either strengthens your anchor or weakens it.

Staying anchored isn't about being perfect.
It's about catching yourself when you start to drift and choosing to pull back toward truth.

> *"Do not conform to the pattern of*
> *this world, but be transformed by*
> *the renewing of your mind."*
> *— Romans 12:2*

How to Stay Anchored

You don't stay steady by accident. God is the anchor holding you in place.

Staying anchored isn't about gripping tighter.
It's about staying connected to the One
who already has you firmly in His hands.

Spending time with God helps you remember that.

Reading your Bible.
Praying.
Listening to worship music.
Even tuning in to podcasts that
point you back to truth.

These moments don't make God closer.
They make *you* more aware of how close He
already is.

They remind you what's true,
even when life gets loud
and your faith feels inconsistent.

And when comparison, fear, or
doubt start pulling at you,
it's okay to pause and ask,
"God, am I drifting?"

Not because He's lost you,
but because He's ready to steady you.

God's faithfulness doesn't depend
on how well you hold on.
He's faithful even when you're
distracted, tired, or unsure.
The anchor hasn't moved.
He hasn't let go.

Sometimes that small pause
is all it takes to remember
you're already held.

Living Differently—On Purpose

Living differently doesn't mean being
judgmental or "better than" anyone.
It means choosing peace over pressure,
honesty over popularity,
and compassion over gossip.
It's about standing for truth
without standing on others.

When people see that steadiness
in you, that quiet confidence,
they'll notice something real.
They'll see the difference God makes
when your heart's anchored in Him.

Consider This

- Where do you feel the pull to "drift"—in your friend group, online, or in how you see yourself?

- What does your anchor look like right now? Strong and steady, or slipping in the current?

- What's one small daily habit (reading a Bible verse, praying, listening to worship music) that could help keep you grounded?

- Who in your life models what it means to live anchored in faith, and what can you learn from them?

Closing Prayer

Dear Lord,
The world feels noisy and confusing sometimes.
It's easy to lose focus and forget
what really matters.
Help me stay anchored in You when everything
around me starts to drift.

Remind me that truth doesn't change,
that peace isn't found in popularity,
and that real strength comes
from staying close to You.

Keep my heart steady and my purpose clear.
When the waves get rough, let my anchor hold.
Amen.

Chapter 11

What Comes After This Life: Living with Eternity in Mind

Let's Talk About What Happens Next

Have you ever noticed that people joke about heaven and hell like they're scenes in a movie? Someone messes up and laughs, "Guess I'm going to hell," like it's going to be one big party. But that's a lie, and a dangerous one.

Hell isn't a celebration.
It's the complete absence of God:
no love, no light, no peace.
And heaven? It's everything our
hearts have been aching for.

It's not some cloud in the sky; it's home,
real, vibrant, and full of joy that never ends.

It's okay to ask questions about what
happens when this life ends.
You're not weird or faithless for wondering.
God invites curiosity because He doesn't
want you to live in fear but in confidence
that this life is just the beginning.

Why We Think About Forever

Even if you've never said it out loud, you've
probably felt it: that quiet sense that there
has to be more than school, work, and
scrolling through days that blur together.
That longing for *more* is eternity
whispering inside you.
God planted it there as a reminder that your life has
purpose far beyond this world.

> *"He has made everything beautiful in its time.*
> *He has also set eternity in the human heart."*
> — *Ecclesiastes 3:11*

That's why no amount of success, likes,
or popularity ever feels like enough.
We were created for something lasting.

What Heaven Will Really Be Like

The Bible gives glimpses of heaven,
enough to stir hope.
Trumpets will sound, announcing Jesus's return.
He'll gather His people home, those who trusted
Him, and there will be no more pain, no more fear,
no more goodbyes.

> *"'He will wipe every tear from their*
> *eyes. There will be no more death'*
> *or mourning or crying or pain."*
> *— Revelation 21:4*

Imagine light so warm it feels like love itself.
Laughter that fills the air.
Peace that finally makes sense.
You see familiar faces, people who believed, and
the moment you see Jesus, you know you're home.

And then you hear the words every heart longs for:

> *"Well done, my good and faithful servant."*
> *— Matthew 25:21 (NLT)*

That's not fantasy; that's promise.

Common Misunderstandings

Heaven isn't a reward for being "good enough."
You can't earn it; it's a gift of grace because
of what Jesus already did for you.
And heaven isn't about sitting on
clouds or becoming angels.
It's real life, restored, full of purpose, creativity, and
relationship the way God meant it to be.

> *"My Father's house has many rooms; if that
> were not so, would I have told you that I am
> going there to prepare a place for you?"*
> *— John 14:2*

There's room for everyone who believes.

And About That "Party in Hell" Lie . . .

The world loves to twist the truth about hell
into something that sounds fun or harmless.
Hell isn't a party with your friends.
It's separation from everything
good, from God Himself.
It's emptiness that never ends.

That's not meant to scare you; it's meant
to show you how much God loves you.
He doesn't want anyone to end up there.
That's why He sent Jesus, to make a way home.

Why Eternity Changes How You Live Now

When you really believe heaven is real,
it changes how you live today.
You start to care less about impressing
people and more about loving them.
You worry less about the temporary and
focus more on what lasts forever.
You begin to live with purpose . . . not panic
. . . because you know where your story ends.

> *"Set your minds on things above,
> not on earthly things."*
> *— Colossians 3:2*

You can trust that the same God preparing your
forever home is also guiding every step right now.

Consider This

- What do you think heaven will *feel* like, not just look like?

- How does knowing eternity is real change what you chase after now?

- If Jesus said, "Well done, my good and faithful servant," what part of your story would you hope He was proud of?

Closing Prayer

Dear Lord,
Thank You for reminding me that
this world isn't all there is.
When I'm caught up in fear or distractions, help
me remember that heaven is real and that You've
already made a place for me there.

Keep me focused on what matters most:
loving people, walking in faith,
and staying close to You.
When I finally see You face-to-face,
let me hear those words: *"Well done."*

Until then, help me live like eternity starts today.
Amen.

Rooted in Faith: What It Means to Grow

When I look back on everything we've
talked about in these pages, one
theme keeps coming up: growth.

Not the kind you can measure by
grades, followers, or achievements,
but the kind that happens quietly,
deep inside your heart.

Growth in faith doesn't always look dramatic.
Sometimes it looks like opening your
Bible even when you don't feel like it.
Or choosing forgiveness when anger feels easier.
Or praying for someone who hurt you because you
finally understand what grace really means.

That's what being *rooted* looks like.
It's steady.
It's patient.
It's real.

Because faith isn't built in big moments;
it's built in everyday ones.
In your car rides.
In your doubts.
In those late-night talks when you're not
sure what to believe but still whisper,
"God, help me trust You."

Where Faith Becomes Your Story

You've learned that believing *in* God
is different than *knowing* Him.
That faith isn't about rules; it's about relationship.
That the people you spend time
with shape your heart.
That love isn't just attraction;
it's respect and patience.
That your life has purpose, even
when you can't see it.
That pain doesn't mean God disappeared;
it means He's shaping something deeper.
That forgiveness is freedom.
That prayer is your direct line to heaven.
That living differently isn't weird;
it's what faith looks like in action.
And that heaven isn't far away;
it's your forever home.

You've learned what it means to walk
with God, not just believe He's real.

And that's where faith stops being a subject
and starts becoming your story.

Stay Rooted

Being rooted in faith doesn't mean
you'll never face storms.
It means when the wind hits, you won't fall apart.
Because your roots go deep,
past feelings, past pressure, past fear.
They're anchored in the One who never changes.

> *"So then, just as you received Christ Jesus
> as Lord, continue to live your lives in him,
> rooted and built up in him, strengthened
> in the faith as you were taught, and
> overflowing with thankfulness."*
> *— Colossians 2:6–7*

You don't have to have it all figured out.
You just have to keep showing up, heart open,
Bible open, willing to grow.

Let God keep writing your story.
Because the more rooted you become,
the more your life will bloom in
ways you never imagined.

Final Reflection

Take a deep breath.
You made it through every page, every question,
every bit of soul-searching.

Now pause and ask yourself:

"What does being rooted in faith look like for me—
today, this week, this year?"

It doesn't have to be perfect.
It just has to be real.

And remember this:
You don't grow closer to God by being flawless.
You grow closer by being *faithful.*

Keep growing.
Keep trusting.
Keep becoming.

Because the best stories God writes always start
with a willing heart.

www.ingramcontent.com/pod-product-compliance
Lightning Source LLC
Chambersburg PA
CBHW021331060726
47591CB00006B/1968